MW00413848

Teacup PIGS

Richard Austin

summersdale

Summersdale Publishers Ltd
46 West Street
Chichester
West Sussex
PO19 1RP
UK

www.summersdale.com

Printed and bound in China

ISBN: 978-1-84953-540-3

Substantial discounts on bulk quantities of Summersdale books are available to corporations, professional associations and other organisations. For details contact Nicky Douglas by telephone: +44 (0) 1243 756902, fax: +44 (0) 1243 786300 or email: nicky@summersdale.com.

To ....

From ....

Introduction

Say hello to the cutest curly-tailed
residents of Pennywell Farm.
Hugo has his deckchair out ready to welcome
the sun, Harry and Holly are getting festive
and Percy is pottering in the vegetable patch.
There's a whole host of adorable piggies
to meet, so what are you waiting for?

Angelica

thinks that every
new visitor deserves
to be greeted with
something sweet.

The bunnies and the butterflies aren't half as cute as these little beauties!

Milo's

favourite things are
straw, potato scraps and
bunny-ear cuddles.

Rain, rain, go away – our
bums are getting wet!

Peter's

a sensible sort,
but he never turns
down a cuddle.

Flo

loves to get out into
the fresh air and
snuffle at the roses.

Herbie's

handy in the kitchen –
and cuter by the pound!

These two sporty snorters
dream of one day
playing for West Ham.

Priscilla,

Queen of Pennywell,
insists on glamming
it up at all times.

Felicity's

always coming up with
new ideas for brightening
the place up a little.

takes to swimming
like a duck to water!

Percy

really enjoys getting his
hooves muddy while
pottering in the garden.

Hilary

isn't much of a snooker
player – she just adores
fuzzy green felt.

Hugo

can't wait to gently
sun his trotters on
a lazy afternoon.

She's got the look!

Claris and Cliff

are keen campers – and
true blue British piggies!

Zoe

loves to take care of her
friends, big or small!

Why does it always
rain on me?

Talula and Tamara

are one fancy double act.

Jake's

always on hand to round
up any misbehaving
members of the
Pennywell family.

Summer

prides herself on her
picture-perfect looks.

Bertram

always gets his five a day!

Harry's

the most dapper
piggy at the farm by
a country mile.

Lottie's

as sharp as a tack and
as cute as a button.

'Oh I do like to be
beside the seaside...'

Thomas

loves to lend a helping
trotter to his fluffy
yellow friends.

Annabel

certainly has a head
for heights.

Winston

is one cool curly-
tailed dude.

Nothing beats a warm,
fluffy cuddle!

Ben and Jerry

are one dynamic
duo when it comes
to outdoor games.

Sophia's

what you might call
'heaven scent'.

Harold

enjoys helping with
the apple harvest – he
gets the leftovers!

There's nothing like
creature comforts.

George

is a curious little chap
and great at making
new friends.

Not many people know it, but pumpkins are actually quite cosy.

Michelle

is a pig who knows
how to party!

just can't do bath time
without his faithful
rubber ducky.

Harry and Holly

are always in a
festive mood!

Bengie's

on the hunt for a
tasty truffle or two.

Prunella

is a pig of fine breeding
and sophistication – and
is uncommonly cute!

The gang's all here!

Freddy's

like a gift that
keeps on giving.

ready to get back to
the pen now, so it's
time to say goodbye...

We hope we can see
you again soon!

Love,

the *Pennywell Teacup Pigs*

xxx

Acknowledgements

The teacup pigs featured in this book have been lovingly bred and maintained by co-owner of Pennywell Farm, **Chris Murray**. He has been breeding the pigs since 1992 and you can visit them in person at the farm in Buckfastleigh, Devon. **www.pennywellfarm.co.uk**

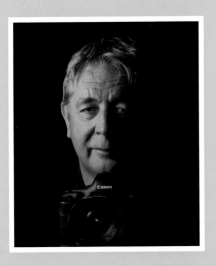

Richard Austin has been a professional news and media photographer for 30 years, working in the newspaper industry in regional, national and the international press. His pictures are also published in various news media the world over.
www.richardaustinimages.com
No animals were harmed at any point during any of the photo shoots.

If you're interested in finding out more about our books, find us on Facebook at **Summersdale Publishers** and follow us on Twitter at **@Summersdale**.

www.summersdale.com